Welc

NAOMI STARKEY

For some people times of solitude are vital for spiritual and emotional health—'water on the dried soil of a pot plant' as Rachel Duff writes ('Very early in the morning...'). Others need to draw their energy and inspiration from interacting with family, friends and colleagues. Whether we welcome or at best tolerate solitude, the challenge is to be open to receive what God may teach us through the experience.

Sister Wendy Beckett is internationally known as an art critic and writer on prayer, yet she spends almost all her days alone in contemplative prayer. In 'The life of solitude', she explores the call to a solitary life—what it involves in practical terms, its spiritual implications. She writes: 'That a life of solitude, without the warmth of human companionship, is completely fulfilling is testimony to the reality of God and what a loving relationship with him can mean.'

Drawing further on insights from the contemplative life, our 'Prayer through the week' for this issue has been written by Sister Stephanie-Thérèse, a member of the Community of the Sisters of the Love of God, an Anglican contemplative order of nuns in Oxford.

In contrast to the men and women for whom solitude is a personal choice, or even obedience to a godly calling, there are those for whom it is (at least initially) an unwelcome situation. Jennifer Rees Larcombe writes about coming to terms with living alone after divorce—and learning to value it as a precious gift. We also hear about two servants of God who were profoundly touched by him during years spent isolated in prison—the Romanian pastor Richard Wurmbrand and the English writer John Bunyan.

Naomi Starkey

1

Text copyright © BRF 2009
Authors retain copyright in their own work
Illustrations copyright © Ian Mitchell, Ray and Corinne Burrows, 2009

Published by
The Bible Reading Fellowship
15 The Chambers, Vineyard
Abingdon, OX14 3FE
United Kingdom
Tel: +44 (0)1865 319700
Email: enquiries@brf.org.uk
Website: www.brf.org.uk

ISBN 978 1 84101 598 9
First published 2009
10 9 8 7 6 5 4 3 2 1 0

Acknowledgments

A catalogue record for this book is available from the British Library

Printed by Gutenberg Press, Tarxien, Malta

Quiet Spaces

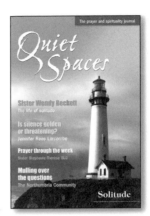

VOLUME 13

CONTENTS

The life of

solitude

Sister Wendy Beckett was born in 1930 and entered a religious order when she was 16. In 1970 she was given permission to pursue a life of solitary contemplation. She lives in a caravan within the enclosure of a monastery.

One is called into solitude to lead a life of prayer

As we know, there are two accounts of creation in the book of Genesis. In the first one, God creates man and woman simultaneously and sets them in their paradise world. The first words that he says to them are 'Be fruitful and multiply, and fill the earth and subdue it' (Genesis 1:28, NRSV). In the second account, God creates Adam and he is the only animate creature in paradise. Apparently, God watches him (we are speaking humanly, of course) and sees that Adam is not happy. 'It is not good that the man should be alone,' says God meditatively (2:18), and in his loving concern for his creature, he creates a world of animals to be companions. Anyone who has loved a dog or cat, or a horse or tortoise or budgie for that matter, knows what companionship animals offer us and knows, too, that it is not enough. God realizes that Adam needs a companion like himself, and so he creates Eve.

Both these stories show, in their own way, how profound our need for community is. This is part of being human, part of our essence. When Jesus taught the apostles how to pray, he began with 'Our Father' and when we say the creed in church, we proclaim 'We believe'. Being human means being inextricably involved with all other men and women. No need to quote John Donne's 'no man is an island'—this is a genetic truth from which we cannot escape. Yet everyone experiences this truth differently. Some people are called to live in the close and immediate community of family; others (the minority who do not marry) will know best the community of friends. But beyond family and friends stretches the world of home, of work, of parish. Even without these tangible and visible signs of community, there is the silent kinship of all human creatures who affect each other just by their existence.

We tread a delicate and sensitive line between acknowledging our communal responsibility for each other and accepting the equally grave responsibility of our singularity. God may be 'our Father' but he is equally 'my Father'. He does not love us in the plural but in the singular. Your love for the Father may encourage and support mine but can never substitute for it. God and I look at one another, and it is completely and uniquely personal. The same is true for the creed. I must bear the weight of my own belief or lack of belief. Is not this the essence of prayer, the relationship with God that can never be shared with another? It seems to me that we are always living as much in solitude as in community, and both obligations must be honoured to the full if we are to mature in Jesus.

God has a different vocation for each of us, however, and there will always be a few whom he summons away from the normal way to holiness, which is communal. Right through Christian history there have been those called to live alone, from the Desert Fathers to contemporary hermits. The very word 'monk' comes from the Greek word for 'one', and in a very true sense monks and nuns, although they live in community, are also dedicated to solitude. Of course, the authority of the Church is behind monastic life, and those called to it have this security.

Many people would prefer to be alone, at least for a while

Those who live in solitude have no one to whom they can turn, except God

What about those living in solitude without the protection of a monastic rule or the enclosure wall?

Anyone who feels called to be a hermit must examine their life situation. God does not reveal himself in visions, but through the actuality of what we are and in our concrete situations in life. There are times (thinking of noisy family reunions or a household full of young children) when many people would prefer to be alone, at least for a while. The test of a vocation is not whether one would like it but whether one needs it. This holds true for any vocation: it is not so

much choice as necessity. However, this is by definition a subjective criterion. It is what 'I' feel, and feelings are notoriously fallible and changeable. If it is a real vocation, there will also be objective criteria. The would-be hermit must have a suitable temperament, by which I mean not overly emotional but able to take the pressure of solitude. Most people need other people—if not the closeness of a partner, then at least friends or even supportive clerics. Those who live in solitude have no one to whom they can turn, except God. Talking things out, expressing fears or guilt or longings, is a luxury unavailable to hermits, and there must be a certain temperamental toughness so that they can flourish without this contact. I sometimes feel that the natural hermit has a rather doughy, porridgy kind of mind, very unexciting.

I think, too, that the prospective hermit must have experienced to the full the purifications of community, as it is very easy to be selfish when you are living alone and have no one but yourself to consider. It seems to me that the ideal preparation for solitude is life in a religious community, where one learns to love a heterogeneous collection of people, not chosen for their compatibility but drawn by a sheer desire to give themselves to God. All communities know misunderstandings and the pain that they bring. It is in giving oneself, despite, or by means of, the inevitable misunderstandings, seeming injustices

or mysterious insensitivities, that the monk or the nun is purified. Not that this is the only way, but it is the only way that I myself have experienced. Community life peels away onion-like layers of selfishness. There may well be many layers left intact, but it is a beginning, a safeguard against the perils of solitude.

In principle, I think, one should go into solitude with a fairly well-stocked mind and a small library. Ideally, there should be access to a larger library, because we cannot love God if our intellect is sluggish. Spiritual reading, theological reading, biblical reading are a necessity, and there may well be a place for lighter reading. We learn much about humanity from the great

Most people need other people

novelists and poets, and recreational reading, too, may have its place. It is a very great privilege to live in solitude, and it must be taken with entire seriousness. To live alone but spend hours in correspondence or even in the gentle occupation of gardening seems to me unworthy of the vocation—a little time, yes, but no more. One is called into solitude to lead a life of prayer, and all one's energies must be directed to that end. How one prays is up to the individual, but that one prays and is bound to prayer and lives for prayer is of the essence.

Complete geographical solitude is rarely possible. There must always be

> Every way of life is only a means to an end, **and the end is always God**

Every Christian…

must have some solitude in his or her life

easy access to the Mass, which is the centre of all prayer and energizes it, infuses it. Quite apart from this, having a church or a monastery that accepts one within its fold represents a great possibility of simplifying life. Asceticism for the hermit consists of a stripping away of inessentials. If one is called to expend all one's energies in prayer, one cannot afford the delicious distractions of, say, cookery. The intensity of the day must vary, or the mind would crack, but there should be an horarium which divides the day into reading and prayer and perhaps some little non-distracting activity (I stress 'little'). Temperamentally, this may be too tough for some people, and everyone who feels called to be a recluse should be allowed a year or two in which this life is tried. Even to

get to this point means that one's circumstances allow for such freedom. There can be innumerable situations in which God makes his will perfectly plain through the inability to embrace such freedoms. Remember that every way of life is only a means to an end, and the end is always God. Any means, any life, lived truthfully and prayerfully leads straight to God. The hermit is privileged but the responsibilities are immense, and it is not a risk to be undertaken lightly.

What hermits have to realize to the depth of their being, almost make their motif, is that they are not called out of the world for their own sake. They are called for the sake of the world. Living in community is the way God has chosen to sanctify his creatures. 'Come away to a deserted place all by yourselves and rest a while,' our Lord told his apostles (Mark 6:31). Very dear to the heart of Archbishop Ramsey were these words of St Augustine: 'We shall rest and we shall see, we shall see and we shall love, we shall love and we shall praise, until that end which is without end.' This 'resting', which enables one to see and love and praise, is not the prerogative of hermits but it is given to them in the fullest of measures.

Every Christian, merely to function as a Christian, must have some solitude in his or her life. Prayer is that solitude. If you believe in the God whom Jesus reveals to us, which is what being a Christian means, then you choose to pray; you are glad to be in the presence of the Father who loves you. Sometimes your prayer may not be physically solitary, but it is always essentially solitary, in that it is you yourself opening your heart to God. Every day we must find a few minutes, maybe no more than ten, to be still and let God take possession of us. Those moments of stillness, of solitude, will orientate our day.

The hermit reinforces for the church the overwhelming significance of God. That a life of solitude, without the warmth of human companionship, is completely fulfilling is testimony to the reality of God and what a loving relationship with him can mean. This relationship is in no way limited by a physical solitude but is one to which every Christian is invited. It says in the Psalms, 'Be still, and know that I am God' (Psalm 46:10)—the implication is that one cannot know unless one is still. In the busy life to which God calls most people, the stillness, although essential, must be brief. The hermit has the strange and frightening vocation of living in this stillness. It confirms the blessedness of God's friendship.

Even if no one knows about the hermit and that they are living with God alone for their support, the hermit life is lived for the community. Contemplative prayer sweetens the atmosphere of the world. It is poured out, silently, invisibly, constantly. Into the murk of human violence and cruelty, into that atmosphere arising from so many sad hearts and darkened places comes this holy air of love and sacrifice and trust in God. We see neither atmosphere, but I am convinced we breathe in both, and it is the atmosphere of prayer (and we are talking here of the intense day-long prayer of the solitary) that sweetens the miasma of human darkness.

I myself am among those whom God has called to this vocation. It seems to me that strong Christians, those who can stand the bustle of ordinary life and through it all look at him with love, are the holy ones. The poor, weak creatures who cannot bear

Yet there is holiness

in every vocation, in that of the married plumber as well as that of the recluse in her caravan

this are called to solitude. In other words, it is the very opposite of a sign of holiness. Yet there is holiness in every vocation, in that of the married plumber as well as that of the recluse in her caravan. Always God has his arms open and his eyes fixed on us with intense affection. Once we have chosen him, he will give himself, and it is he who will make clear the circumstances in which he will take possession. God will not be denied the expression of his love. All that is asked of us is to be ready to receive him. ∎

To be
a pilgrim

Mark Woods is a Baptist minister. After studying literature at university, he had pastorates in Bristol and Alvechurch, Worcestershire. He moved to 'The Baptist Times' in 2002. Now its editor, he particularly enjoys writing art, TV and theatre reviews.

He has to be brave and thoughtful **as well as faithful**

Terry Waite, the Archbishop of Canterbury's special envoy to the Middle East, knew more about solitude than most of us. For him, it was not a matter of choice: kidnapped during a visit to Beirut in an attempt to secure the release of Western hostages, he spent nearly five years virtually in solitary confinement.

During that time, he received a postcard from a woman he had never met. It showed John Bunyan in prison. He was holding a pen and gazing across Bedford, where he spent twelve years in prison for preaching without a licence. 'What a lucky fellow,' thought Terry Waite ruefully at the time; Bunyan had a pen, at least, and he was in his own town, not thousands of miles from home.

Neither of these men chose their solitude willingly, but both of them were able to turn their experiences to good. Terry Waite wrote *Taken on Trust* (Hodder & Stoughton, 1993), a deeply honest and moving account of his trials, and he learnt profound spiritual lessons from his experience. It was during his twelve years in Bedford jail that Bunyan wrote *The Pilgrim's Progress*, a work that has shaped the spirituality of the Protestant part of the Church ever since.

Parts of it, if we are honest, are a little dry; the 17th century was steeped in a rather spiky theology, and even Bunyan was a keen controversialist. But *The Pilgrim's Progress* is written from a full and generous heart, and Bunyan's desire was to help his readers on their journey to the Celestial City. Some have claimed it to be the most widely read book in the English language. Its turns of phrase and its characters have entered our everyday speech, whether we know where they come from or not. It has been translated into more than 200 languages, and it has never been out of print since it was first published—the first part in 1678 and the second in 1684.

The Pilgrim's Progress speaks to us today, not just in its homely advice and spiritual wisdom, but in the way it teaches us to think about our lives and perhaps most of all in the circumstances of its writing.

There are, I believe, three things it has to say to us. First, it tells us that life is a journey, and what happens to us on the way is to be seen in the light of the goal of that journey, which is heaven. Christian, the hero of the first book, becomes aware that he carries a great burden and that his city is in peril; literally, he runs for his life. The trials and temptations that he faces are attempts to make him turn from the straight and narrow way. Doubting Castle, the Giant Despair, Vanity Fair—we know them all so well because they're real, and we face them ourselves. Christian is helped by his fellow pilgrims, but he has

Both of them were able to turn their experiences to good

He learnt profound spiritual lessons from his experience

to be brave and thoughtful as well as faithful, and keep his eyes on the goal.

Nowadays there is a way of looking at the world known as postmodernism. One of its central ideas is that there is no big story that shapes the world we live in. There are just our own desires and our own choices, and life means what we say it means, day by day and moment by moment.

This worldview contains some valuable insights, but a book like *The Pilgrim's Progress* invites us to look at the world quite differently. The things that happen to us have a meaning. God speaks to us through them, and they are incidents on the road to the goal he has prepared. Life is not random; it has a point—and God provides us with guides through the wilderness: scripture and the company of faithful friends. We are not aimless wanderers, we are pilgrims, and our goal is ahead of us.

John Bunyan did not choose his solitude but it brought him a great gift: the time to look at his own heart through the lens of his faith, and the ability to understand that his own story was one thread in the great tapestry God is making.

The second thing we learn from *The Pilgrim's Progress* is the importance of other people. The beginning of Book I is very sobering: Christian begins to run from his home, and his wife and children cry out for him to return. 'But,' writes Bunyan, 'the man put his fingers in his ears and ran on, crying "Life, life, eternal life."' The second book brings Christian's family to the Celestial City as well, but this is a stark reminder of the choice each of us must make alone.

Being responsible for our own choices does not mean that we can be solitary pilgrims, even if circumstances have given us too much of our own company. Solitude makes some people turn in on themselves and become the most important person in their own world. John Bunyan resisted the temptation

> One of its central ideas is that there is no big story that shapes the world we live in

We are not aimless wanderers, we are pilgrims, and our goal is ahead of us

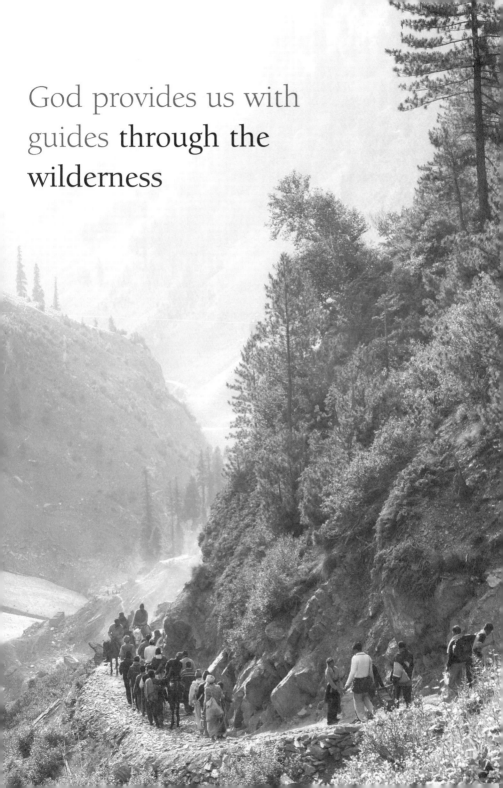

God provides us with guides **through the wilderness**

to be selfishly introspective or to make himself the hero of his book. He filled its pages with other people—the good, the bad and the ugly. Pliable and Obstinate, Mr Worldly Wiseman, Talkative and Ignorance are not good company, to say the least, but it is in talking with them and learning to resist their arguments and examples that Christian wins through. Faithful is his companion and is steadfast in his martyrdom; Hopeful sustains him to the very end. All the vices and virtues, the hindrances and helps in *The Pilgrim's Progress* are very human, and they stand for real encounters with real people.

Other people teach us things even when we do not realize we are learning them: 'As iron sharpens iron, so one man sharpens another' (Proverbs 27:17, NIV). Imagining that all we need to do in order to grow in our Christian faith is to pray and read our Bibles at home is very foolish. G.K. Chesterton wrote in *The Sign of the Broken Sword*: 'When will people understand that it is useless for a man to read his Bible unless he also reads everybody else's Bible?'

> ## What happens to us on the way is to be **seen in the light of the goal of that journey**

© Mikhail Levit. Used under licence from Shutterstock, Inc.

> [Other people] place us within the network of human contact that is society

Third, *The Pilgrim's Progress* reminds us that we are never so alone that we are without God. We are not, by nature, solitary beings, and enforced solitude can be very damaging. Indeed, our word 'idiot' comes from a Greek word meaning 'one alone' or 'private person'. It is not normal to have no interaction whatsoever with other people. They tell us who we are; they remind us that we matter; they place us within the network of human contact that is society.

It takes a particular kind of person to bear long periods of solitary confinement in prison, like

Bunyan. While some of us cannot cope with our own company at all and are only energized and fulfilled by being with others, most of us like some time out, to be on our own.

There are plenty of people—too many—who, because of age or infirmity or lack of resources, live lonely lives and lack the reassurance of their significance that comes from friendship or the care of a life partner. There are not enough people in their lives, and it is hard for them to feel valued. No one should diminish or denigrate such an experience, and Christians should have a particular care for those who may be going through such a time. In the end, though, we are worth something because we are loved by God, as his children, not because of anything given or withheld by other people.

In one of his essays, the great historian Lord Macaulay bracketed together John Bunyan and John Milton as the two most imaginative minds of the later 17th century. Milton was another author and poet who lost a glittering political career after choosing the wrong side in the Civil War and then lost his sight and became blind. One of his last poems was a sonnet, 'On his Blindness', in which he wrestles with what he believes is his uselessness. But God, he realizes, has all the servants he needs: 'God doth not need / Either man's work, or His own gifts…' The poem concludes, 'They also serve who only stand and wait.'

We may not be able to do for God, or for ourselves, what we would wish, but we are still held within God's purposes and can trust in his goodness. ∎

His own story was one thread in the great tapestry God is making

15

Safe hands?

After serving with her family for eight years in West Asia, Meryl Leach now lives in Bedford and works for Interserve as their International Prayer Coordinator. She divides her time between this role, her family responsibilities and involvement with her local church.

It can be tempting to look around at other pots that God is making

It was a rainy evening and I'd escaped for a snatch of solitude. The low tide enabled me to drive over the exposed causeway to Holy Island—a place of quietness, steeped in Christian history. For me a walk alone in a beautiful place is often where I feel close to God—just me, absorbing the beauty of creation and allowing him to speak to me through it. As I walked towards the distant castle, the sun fought a battle with the rain and ahead of me I saw a rainbow. I stopped to capture it on film, and when I realized that I could actually see the rainbow's end touching the grass near the shore, I decided to walk to the place. Not expecting a pot of gold, I was nevertheless surprised to see an unusual gathering. There on the ground was a collection of 'treasures' from the sea: pieces of sea glass, shards of pottery and simple stones. Displayed in a rough circle, these chosen pieces awaited discovery. I was touched; it seemed somehow a significant find although I wasn't sure why.

A few weeks later, back in the regular routines, that solitary walk seemed far away. The day was a normal one and I was making plans, getting on with the everyday tasks of family life, when my world was suddenly plunged into chaos. My husband told me that he had lost his faith and had decided that God no longer existed. As we were both full-time Christian workers serving overseas, the implications of his words had far-reaching consequences —like the toppling of the first in a line of dominos. I felt as if the sky had fallen.

I thought back to my summer. We had been back in the UK, sharing about our work. I had talked about how God was challenging me through the verse in Isaiah 64:8 (NIV): 'Yet, O Lord, you are our Father. We are the clay, you are the potter; we are all the work of your hand.'

I was familiar with the picture of God as a potter. Recently, though, during a time of quiet reflection I had felt that God was challenging me afresh to let him shape me. The potter will often find some

It seemed somehow a significant find

imperfections in the clay as he shapes his pot. In order to make the best possible pot he will need to remove those imperfections. Sometimes he needs to reshape the pot completely.

God as the potter is a wonderful picture. He uses his creative power in our lives to make us into something more beautiful. We, as clay, are formed in his hands but, unlike clay, we have a choice. Sometimes we are willing and long to be shaped but at other times we resist his touch. Why is this? I think there are a number of reasons: fear, complacency and comparison with others.

Fear is one of the biggest things that can hold back growth in our lives. It can creep in through lots of small ways, or it can engulf and paralyse us. We don't trust God fully and allow fear to keep us from

17

© zahorec. Used under licence from Shutterstock, Inc.

Being clay in God's hands feels vulnerable

reaching our highest potential. God doesn't abandon us but he does long to be allowed to help us in a fearful situation.

I know just how easily fear can creep in. In the past year, we had bought a car after years of using public transport. It was a whole new challenge, driving in the country where we were then living. Rules seemed few and a short journey was often eventful for the wrong reasons. Just as I was beginning to enjoy driving, a car pulled out of a side turning without looking and just drove into me, which was a real blow

to my newfound confidence. I realized that I had a choice: I could either give in to my fear or get through it. Through prayers, both my own and those of others, through listening to worship music and through sheer determination I gradually worked through. God helped me regain confidence—but give me England to drive in any day! It is not easy to take a step of faith when the outcome is unknown.

Another way that fear can hold us back is by making us feel vulnerable. Most of us enjoy a sense of being in control, of using our skills. We become accomplished at avoiding situations outside our comfort zones, yet this may be exactly where God wants us to be so that he can mould us. I experienced vulnerability when I moved to a country where I couldn't speak the language and didn't know the culture. None of my dearly held skills were worth very much when I couldn't communicate. It was an uncomfortable situation. Yes, being clay in God's hands feels vulnerable, yet when we allow him to work through us, we find he can be trusted.

Complacency leads us to grow content with something that is less than God's best for us. Our lives become so busy that we stop longing to grow. We get in a rut and keep going with the same old things. We may know that there is stuff in our lives that isn't pleasing to God, but somehow we never get around to dealing with it. Isaiah 55:8–9 says: '"My thoughts are not your thoughts, neither are your ways my ways," declares the Lord. "As the heavens are higher than the earth, so are my ways higher than your ways and my thoughts than your thoughts."' We need to expect more and pray for God to share some of his thoughts and ways with us. We need to take that first step out of our comfortable rut.

It can be tempting to look around at other pots that God is making and think, 'If only God had made me like him or her, I could be so much more effective.' We don't realize that by comparing ourselves with others in this way we are actually expressing dissatisfaction with our Creator's work. It can be a real obstacle to growth if we reject the pot into which God is shaping us. 1

Corinthians 12:18–20 reminds us that we are all different parts of one body. We each have a role to play, and knowing and accepting that role is a step towards allowing the potter to work in our lives. God wants to develop our full potential in him; he will not toss us out and take up another pot.

Our lives become so busy that we **stop longing to grow**

In looking at the pot, we mustn't forget the potter. As he works on us, many of God's qualities shine through.

- His watchfulness: a potter needs to concentrate on the job and not be distracted. He can't make a pot while watching football or looking to see what others are doing. Psalm 121:2–3 speaks of God's watchfulness: 'My help comes from the Lord, the Maker of heaven and earth. He will not let your foot slip—he who watches over you will not slumber.'

- His creativity: he sees the potential in each lump of clay and puts his creative energy into forming it. Scripture tells us that we are made in God's image, that the creator God puts something of himself into each pot he makes. I like the thought of God standing back with a satisfied sigh as he takes pleasure in his creation.
- His redemptive nature: God's hands are able to remove our imperfections and reshape our

---

... stripped away some of the things I had **taken for granted**

---

clay. His job as a potter is ongoing. Our lives are unique, created and redeemed by him. Philippians 3:20–21 says: 'Our citizenship is in heaven. And we eagerly await a Saviour from there, the Lord Jesus Christ, who, by the power that enables him to bring everything under his control, will transform our lowly bodies so that they will be like his glorious body.' What a wonderful process—becoming more like Christ!

- His love: God's hands on our lives are hands of love. Think about the way that the hands of the potter

are in direct contact with the clay while it is on the wheel. If he takes his hands away, that gentle pressure will be lost and the pot will take on a shape of its own. He stays with the clay, clay that will dirty his hands and resist his forming at times. He waits for us to allow him to work.

I was challenged by the insights God gave me into the verse from Isaiah, as I have already said. I wasn't quite sure what needed to be reshaped in my life, but I knew deep down that I had to express my willingness to God to allow him to work. I prayed that he would form me into the pot he wanted me to be, although I had no idea at the time what that reshaping would involve.

As I deal with the present pain and confusion of my life, God is very close. He has stripped away some of the things I had taken for granted, which were my security. I experience a new, unwelcome solitude in my life, but he has never left me. He has taken me back to that walk to the rainbow's end and showed me that I am his gathered treasure, tossed about by the sea yet becoming formed, not smashed. His promises are over me like that rainbow's end shining over the collection of stones and glass, giving me many reassurances of his ongoing work in my life. I write now from a place of uncertainty, having no guarantees of a 'happy ending', but I do know that I am in safe hands. ■

Is silence
golden or threatening?

Jennifer Rees Larcombe has a fruitful and long-established prayer, healing, speaking and writing ministry, most recently focused on helping people adjust to pain, loss and trauma. Her most recent book, 'Journey into God's Heart' (Hodder & Stoughton, 2006), tells her life story.

As I unlocked my front door, pulling my case in after me, I sighed with relief as the silence welcomed me home. The last few days had been a whirl of travelling, speaking, praying with people in distress and making polite conversation with hosts and their families. Now I could switch off, make a cup of tea and enjoy the undemanding quality of solitude. As I flopped on to the sofa, I suddenly realized that I was experiencing a miracle. A few years ago, coming

... enjoy the undemanding quality of solitude

home to an empty house would have resulted in tears of loneliness and self-pity as my memory replayed happy voices and laughter from the past. Silence used to feel anything but welcoming.

Like many others I had always thought, 'I could never live alone.' My first 23 years were spent in a Christian community with an extended family of 35. During my marriage, we often

For the first time in my life, I was alone...

had live-in visitors, as well as our six children and their rabble of friends. Then, when our youngest went to university, my husband left me for someone else, and for the first time in my life I was alone. The desolation was unbearable. I had vowed to love and cherish him until 'death did us part' 30 long and happy years before;

now, I would probably always be alone. The thought made me feel suicidal.

A recent survey asked the question, 'What do you fear most?' Loneliness was high on the list of answers. Right back in Genesis 2:18 we read, 'The Lord God said, "It is not good for the man to be alone"'(NIV), so maybe he did not design us to live separately. Of course there are people who actually *choose* to be single for religious reasons or because God created them with the kind of inner strength that does not need other people. However, when 'aloneness' is thrust on us against our will, many of us struggle.

We often have to put up with jokes about 'being left on the shelf' or jollied along by being told, 'Never mind, dear, you'll soon get a new man in your life.' It is not just that the rest of the world sees us as 'different' or an object of pity; deep down we resent it because we never wanted life to be this way. Maybe we always thought we would get married someday and have a family, but we have to smile our way through the weddings of all our friends and the arrival of their babies, while inside a

little voice whispers, 'God, why are you leaving me out of all this?' Perhaps we lose a spouse or very close friend through death or, as in my case, desertion, and silently the voice shouts, 'This isn't fair, God! You let me down.' Sometimes this voice, which we try so hard to stifle, is not arguing with God but accusing *us*: 'No one wants to share your life because you're too boring or unattractive.' Or maybe it says, 'It's all *your* fault! You always mess up your relationships.' For me the 'voice' accused the person who had abandoned me: 'How dare he sentence me to life alone!'

This inner restlessness often causes us to stop trusting God with our lives. Instead, we take matters into our own hands by finding someone else to fill the empty void. I have seen so many people dashing into relationships that turn out to be a lot more painful than solitude could ever have been. Sometimes an older person decides to pool their resources with one of their grown-up children and they buy a house together, large enough to share, or create a 'granny-annexe'. When it does not work out happily, their finances are so intertwined that the whole family are trapped in a miserable situation—all because living alone felt like an impossible challenge.

It took me a long time to move from feeling outraged by the prospect of 'aloneness' to appreciating it so much that I would not dream of swapping it for any other way of life. Through my work as a counsellor, I

have watched many other people make that transition, too, so I know it is possible.

It was a phrase in an old poem written by the missionary Amy Carmichael that helped me profoundly: 'In acceptance lieth peace.' Acceptance is not 'giving in' with a sigh of resignation, like a powerless victim. Acceptance says, 'I never wanted or planned this kind of life, but I am choosing to stop regretting the things I've lost and I'm going to enjoy as much as possible of this life that I have.'

When 'aloneness' is thrust on us against our will, **many of us struggle**

Inner restlessness often causes us to **stop trusting God with our lives**

Before I reached that point, I used to get mad with well-meaning friends who quoted Romans 8:28 at me: 'In all things God works for the good of those who love him.' I didn't want to be 'done good to', I just wanted my husband back. Then, very gradually,

23

In order to access those blessings **I had to embrace singleness**

I began to realize that God had actually allowed all this to happen. He had not planned it to be this way but he wanted to use it to bring all kinds of good things into my life. In order to access those blessings I had to embrace singleness until such a time as he changed my situation. I needed to forgive my ex-husband and also myself for my part in the failure of our marriage. Then I had to 'forgive' God for not answering my prayers in the way I wanted.

Forgiveness and acceptance made it possible for me to begin to enjoy the good things about living alone. And there are a lot of good things! Some of mine are *not* having to watch sport on TV, eating what I like when I like, and filling the house with my favourite music! This decision to enjoy life is vital and little things matter, like planning and cooking 'proper' meals and sitting down to enjoy them. I let myself watch half an hour of a DVD while I eat, as it makes me 'switch off' in the same way that conversation would. Hobbies and interests are important because they fill evenings and weekends, which feel strangely empty when your life doesn't have to fit round anyone else. Happiness is a decision, but you have to work at it by planning treats to which you can look forward. Friends are probably more important to a single person than to a couple, but maintaining them and making new ones takes effort. It is a temptation to think, 'Oh, they wouldn't want me,' or 'I'm too tired to bother.'

Of course, the best thing about living alone is the way it develops your relationship with God—because there is no one else but him to please or consider. People often talk about 'their other half' and, when you don't have one, it can make you feel like only half a person. When we share the double yoke with Jesus that he talks about in Matthew 11:28–30, he becomes our 'better half' in a very real way. Soon after my husband left,

I rediscovered Isaiah 54:5: 'Your Maker is your husband.' At the time the practical business side of life was a nightmare but that verse felt like God's promise to take care of all these things just as my husband had done so efficiently. I have never lacked anything I needed ever since and I have learnt to depend on God for every detail of my life.

Far more important than physical things were my emotional needs. I longed to be loved unconditionally and valued for who I was because, on a human level, I felt totally unloved and 'scrap-heaped'. Gradually I've come to appreciate just how much God loves me and enjoys my constant company. Now he is the one with whom I speak the moment I wake, chat as I have breakfast and share the joy of a walk with the dog. He is there waiting for me in the empty house but he has also been with me all the time I've been out!

> ... the deep satisfaction of allowing God to fill our solitude

While we are constantly trying to find a human being who will share our lives and meet our emotional or material needs, we never discover the deep satisfaction of allowing God to fill our solitude. ∎

Lost and found

I missed him when the sun began to bend;
I found him not when I had lost his rim;
With many tears I went in search of him,
Climbing high mountains which did still ascend,
And gave me echoes when I called my friend;
Through cities vast and charnel-houses grim,
And high cathedrals where the light was dim,
Through books and arts and works without an end,
But found him not—the friend whom I had lost.
And yet I found him—as I found the lark,
A sound in fields I heard but could not mark;
I found him nearest when I missed him most;
I found him in my heart, a life in frost,
A light I knew not till my soul was dark.

GEORGE MACDONALD (1824–1905)

Very early in the morning...

Rachel Duff trained as a nurse but now works for her local city council with vulnerable and needy families as a Family Centre Worker. Together with her husband, Mike, and their two children, she has recently returned from working in Indonesia with CMS and they now live in Southsea, Hampshire.

The day dawns sunny and warm. The early morning call to prayer, echoing across rooftops from mosque to mosque, has died away. A few people walk past the house on their way to work or the market. It is still, peaceful and quiet. I get out of bed, the pale tiles cool beneath my feet, and pad through to the kitchen to make a cup of tea. The cat winds herself around my ankles and together we go out on to the porch and sit blinking into the garden, the sunshine and the new day.

Some months later, on the other side of the world, the harsh bleep of the alarm pulls me from sleep. It is dark and chilly. I get out of bed feeling for slippers, dressing-gown.

Twenty minutes later I leave a sleeping house and head with the dog through the damp streets, a scarf snugly wrapped around my neck, across the common to the war memorial and the sea. The dog and I stand, with the wind blowing ears and hair, and look into the new day.

Finding times of quiet in my days can be a challenge but, when I do, the words of Psalm 23 describe well the way God restores my perspective and nurtures me in all the busyness of life. It's like pausing to breathe slowly in and out and stop for a moment: 'He makes me lie down in green pastures, he leads me beside quiet waters, he restores my soul' (Psalm 23:2, NIV).

While my life circumstances have changed dramatically as my family and I have moved across continents, each day still brings its own demands and commitments, and some days seem to have more room than others. For me, however, times of solitude are like water on the dried soil of a pot plant. These times soak into me, give me perspective and, as the psalmist says, restore my soul. They are also a choice.

While in Indonesia, I once complained to a friend that I missed the walks by the sea that I had enjoyed in England. She challenged me by asking where my 'walks by the sea' could be in the busy, hot, polluted, landlocked city where we now lived. I knew I had to find such a space in my week because otherwise my soul would become parched and mean. So I found the early morning sun on our porch, a quiet corner in a café with a cup of coffee, a solitary walk around an air-conditioned shopping mall where a white face did not draw so many comments.

He retreated from the activity of his ministry in order to be alone with God

In Mark 1:35, we read that Jesus 'got up, left the house and went off to a solitary place, where he prayed'. He retreated from the activity of his ministry in order to be alone with God. In the early days of our time in Indonesia, we expended so much energy in everyday living, from sterilizing the vegetables and finding our way around to talking in another language, that we quickly became exhausted and emotionally drained.

God restores my perspective and nurtures me in all the busyness of life

Psalm 46:1 says that 'God is our refuge and strength, an ever-present help in trouble'. Being out of our comfort zone meant that we called upon God much more often as our own skills and Western ways of coping failed us in the face of an alien culture. Spending time alone with God, talking in English(!), gave us the strength we needed to face the ongoing challenges.

After we had been in Indonesia for about three months, I became ill with food poisoning, which increased in severity over a few days. Eventually it became obvious that I was very ill and needed to go to hospital. We had to find someone to look after the children, borrow a car (there is no 999 service) and then stop to get some cash to pay for the treatment. By the time we got to the hospital I was delirious and talking nonsense. Mike, my husband, did not have the language skills to convey the history of the illness and watched me being wheeled away down a long corridor, cockroaches scuttling to the sides. He was helpless to know what to do. In England, it would all have been so simple—we would have known whom to call; we would hardly have felt we needed to pray. In Indonesia prayer was all we had. We called out to God for understanding and healing—and, in due course, I recovered.

One of the exciting elements of living in a new culture was that we found new aspects of our characters revealed, often in surprising ways. One of these ways was discovering how we adapted our fast-paced Western lives to the flexible timekeeping of our new home. After four years in Indonesia, it was a shock to arrive back in the UK and find people too busy to have us round for the next six weeks. We once again live in 'diary land'; times of solitude rarely come naturally into the day and, if they do, we often overlook them. Instead, we need to seek them out and consciously make use of them.

I am currently lucky enough to live in a large Victorian vicarage, with space to make the smallest bedroom at the top of the house into a prayer room. The physical activity of climbing the stairs to this place of retreat helps me to shed the immediate distractions of the day. As I open the door, it is as if I am entering God's place, a space where God and I can spend time together. It is where I am more receptive to his word. Here I drop my shoulders, breathe deeply and sit with him a while in the absence of others. This is where I lie down in green pastures, beside quiet waters, and where my heavenly Father restores my soul.

What can we do when such a space is not available to us? What do we do when we lose a familiar 'quiet space', as when I could no longer walk by the sea following the move abroad? As a child, I attended St Hilda's boarding school in Whitby, run by the sisters of the Order of the Holy Paraclete. On end-of-term train journeys from school to King's Cross, we would often be accompanied by one of the sisters. In the midst of a busy train carriage, surrounded by excited schoolgirls, she would take out her prayer book and retreat into time with God. I still remember the sense of space around her during

those times as she encountered God while sitting on a train.

It takes practice but, as I found in Indonesia, we can choose to create quiet spaces in daily life, in the most unlikely of settings. While waiting at traffic lights in the car, in the dentist's waiting room, preparing a meal, doing the ironing, walking to work, we can open ourselves up to the spirit of God and find an oasis of solitude in the midst of all that we do. Martin Luther

I still remember the
sense of space around her

We can choose to create quiet spaces in daily life, in the **most unlikely of settings**

said he was so busy that he could not spend fewer than three hours a day in prayer. This seems like a mountain of the highest proportions to most of the rest of us, who tend to spend less time with God the busier we are. Even so, there is something very attractive about those who spend time in solitude with God, a sense of wisdom and peace that many of us merely strive for. Of course, we can also struggle with God, and a time of solitude may actually be when we shout out our hurts and anger at him. Indeed, Jesus came before God in the garden of Gethsemane in anguish about what lay ahead for him (Luke 22:41–44), but as he prayed he gave himself up to God's will and found the strength to continue his journey to Calvary.

For many people, myself included, solitude is an essential part of life. We

We were all silenced by the horror of what we saw

We may struggle to keep our daily lives in balance, but we sense the need for time apart with God

may struggle to keep our daily lives in balance, but we sense the need for time apart with God and relish the chance to lay down the tools of work and all other distractions and withdraw into solitude. For others, however, solitude may not be

welcome. I have a friend who finds herself increasingly alone due to a debilitating illness. She wishes it were otherwise, but, while she could sink into loneliness, it seems to me that she chooses to have an attitude of solitude instead. And in that choice God speaks powerfully to her. She continues to live with the 'why' of her illness but she increasingly reveals God to her friends.

One abiding memory I have of Indonesia is watching the sun rise over the smoking rim of Mount Bromo, an active volcano on the island of Java. A large crowd of us stood waiting for the early morning light to reveal the mountain to us. There was a general murmur of conversation, but as the oranges, reds and blues of the sunrise grew brighter, we were silenced by the awesome beauty of what we saw. Two years earlier, I had been standing together with others on a medical team, looking over the devastation that the tsunami had caused to the city of Banda Aceh in northern Sumatra. We were all silenced by the horror of what we saw. Both were examples of collective solitude as group members individually processed the scene before them and met with God in the beauty and the destruction, finding him in the midst of both.

James 4:8 says, 'Come near to God and he will come near to you.' My experience is that I need to choose to come to God, to find that he restores my soul in the midst of the everyday, whatever that day might bring. ∎

The Path of *Celtic Prayer*

Praying without ceasing

We sometimes wonder about Paul's admonition to pray without ceasing (1 Thessalonians 5:17, KJV). Can we do it? Is it really possible? One thing is certain, the key is to see prayer as something we are instead of something we do. Long, wandering prayer is that sort of defining prayer. It is the lifelong journey between the 'Our Father in heaven' and 'We ask these things in the name of Christ.' The life of pilgrimage praying isn't merely punctuated by prayer. The pilgrimage is the prayer. The *peregrini* weren't going somewhere to pray, they were praying as they went, wherever they went. They were pilgrims without a shrine. Life wasn't a destination; life was the journey.

As he travelled the Hebrides, Calvin Miller sensed God calling him to a fresh adventure in prayer, learning from the spiritual traditions of places such as Iona. In 'The Path of Celtic Prayer' (BRF, 2008), he sets out six principles of prayer drawn from his reflection on Celtic spirituality. Here are some of his thoughts on 'long, wandering prayer'.

See prayer as something we are
instead of something we do

Photograph © Mark Graves. Used under licence from Shutterstock, Inc.

They never really 'arrived', so they never stopped praying.

Whatever our apparent earthly destinations, our life itself is a pilgrimage. Once we understand that we will never 'arrive', we can remain in a continual state of prayer. This doesn't mean we are always talking to God. The fullest definition of long, wandering prayer is journeying in the presence of the triune God. Even when our hearts are not wrapped (or rapt) in conversation with the Almighty, we are yet in his presence.

... journeying in the presence of the triune God

... our life journey of long, wandering prayer can be shaped by unimaginable encounters with the three-personed God

Whether we talk or listen to God, we are to live in the lifelong abundance of his presence. This sort of presence is the bedrock of long, wandering prayer. This is why my long trek to work and back is fulfilling. God and I are not always in verbal contact, but his presence is real. Thus I am able to define my morning commute as a long, wandering prayer.

What is the basis of our union with God? Why does his presence endure? The answer to both questions is God's Son. The poet D. Gwenallt Jones calls Calvary 'the binding place of God and man'. God, in his grace, redeemed us through his Son's incarnation, life, death and resurrection. There is a yearning to make peace—to become one—in God's love, and in Christ our yearnings to be united with God are satisfied. Here the yearnings of the great Trinity and the needy pilgrim meet.

Earthbound help for the pilgrim

Prayer need not be a solo trip. According to James 5:13–16, the needy should pray with and for each other. Indeed, this is why God gave us the Church. Brendan did not navigate the seas alone. Likewise, there's room on our journey for soul friends (or prayer partners). When we engage in long, wandering prayer with such friends, we discover a broader dimension of union with Christ. As an ancient Jewish wise man said:

A faithful friend is a secure shelter;
whoever finds one, finds a treasure.
A faithful friend is beyond price;
there is no measure of his worth.
A faithful friend is an elixir of life,
found only by those who fear the Lord.
ECCLESIASTICUS 6:14–16 (REB)

The Celtic model is not one of short-term or occasional friendship, but a daily commitment throughout life. The 19th-century writer Dinah Maria Mulock Craik wrote of this kind of friendship (in *A Life for a Life*, 1859):

Oh the comfort, the inexpressible comfort of feeling safe with a person; having neither to weigh thoughts nor measure words, but pouring them all right out, just as they are, chaff and grain together; certain that a faithful hand will take and sift them, keep what is worth keeping, and then, with the breath of kindness, blow the rest away.

Life can be viewed as one long prayer journey. If we follow the example of the *peregrini*, the implications for our worldview are enormous. Their prayer life and mission work were never finished. In fact, most of these Celtic mariners didn't return home because they saw themselves as perpetual exiles. How can we regain our lost sense of pilgrimage?

The temporary service and the temporary shrine

In Chaucer's *Canterbury Tales* we find a group of pilgrims journeying to the shrine of St Thomas at Canterbury. Once there, we assume they would have passed the time in prayers and vigils, but soon their spiritual experience would be over and they would have to trudge back to their home lives. This, I'm afraid, is how most of us view pilgrimage.

... I am able to define my morning commute as a long, wandering prayer

Life can be viewed as one long prayer journey

The *peregrine* pilgrimage was different. For these sailors, the horizon was the call. Every island they touched was a place to discover something new about God. We need to view their voyages as metaphorical in nature. Just as Brendan's travel was informed by these wild experiences, so our life journey of long, wandering prayer can be shaped by unimaginable encounters with the three-personed God.

What kind of Christ would call Brendan into the wilds of the sea, where the waves pounded and the winds blew? What does this Christ look like? Not the Christ of the high cathedrals of Europe. No! This is a seagoing Christ, a Christ who beckons without compass. He bids his dear followers put out to sea and trust the currents as the channel of God's will. ■

Music for the soul:

Musical solitude

Gordon Giles is vicar of St Mary Magdalene's Church, Enfield, north London. He contributes to BRF's 'New Daylight' notes and has also written 'The Music of Praise' (2002), 'The Harmony of Heaven' (2003) and 'O Come, Emmanuel' (2005) for BRF.

Where there is music, you are never alone. This is why so many use personal stereos and MP3 players—to avoid the isolation we feel when travelling or walking the streets. While there are often lots of people about, a crowd can still be a lonely, even threatening context, in the midst of which we may feel more isolated than protected. We choose to enter another world of solitude, that inner space between the headphones where there is just us and the music.

Some people use music to remove other sounds around them. In doing so, they are probably not listening to it, paying attention to the movement of notes, following lyrics or enjoying harmony, structure or melodic variation. All music can be treated as 'musak', sound intended to be heard but not given direct attention. 'Musak' was conceived by the Musak Corporation of America, and is intended to engender a particular mood, conducive to shopping, working or relaxation. It is the 'easy listening' in the background while you push your shopping trolley; it is the classical music used on Newcastle's metro stations to deter vandals and it is played as you board an aeroplane, to help you forget the tremendous racket the engines make even when stationary. You are not supposed to listen to it, but you can hear it, and it influences you, an aural 'smell', like the bread and coffee wafted around supermarkets.

If it is true that we 'hear' a lot of music but rarely listen to it, as we either allow or are forced to let our attention wander, where does that leave the composer? Although the Muzak Corporation commissioned special music for its purposes, most music these days can be used as muzak. When Beethoven and Brahms composed, they expected people to sit down and listen, to appreciate the

technical brilliance, emotional depth and inner structures of their offerings. I often wonder what these men would have thought about their music being used to calm delinquents or sell butter!

Traditionally, composers wrote music for the glory of God or for themselves or sometimes just for cash, but they also wrote in order to communicate something to which their listeners might relate. Most music written in the West before 1800 was intended either to celebrate or to comment upon an aspect of the divine, such as creation or

Composers wrote music **for the glory of God**

redemption. Some works were an expression of praise, intended as vehicles through which others could offer worship. Nowadays, most music is not composed with the intention of glorying God—doing so would not occur to the composers—and music of all generations finds its way on to little boxes with minuscule loudspeakers, which, despite their smallness, provide solitude even on a crowded train.

Since solitude need not involve silence, and true silence does not really exist, music has become a spiritual panacea, a means to escape the world. John Cage, an American avant-garde composer who died in 1992, wrote a book called *Silence*, in which he reminded his readers that if you put yourself in a soundproof room you cannot hear 'nothing': you will hear the beat of your own heart and other bodily functions. He also wrote a work called 4'33" to prove the point. A 'performance' involves the 'performer' doing nothing, but the audience pays attention to the sounds that occur in the concert hall during those four and a half minutes.

We cannot escape the world: our minds may try but our bodies will not let us. John Cage did not know about 'noise-cancelling' headphones, which use a microphone to detect extraneous sound and electronically replace it with digital silence (making the listening experience pleasanter by 'pasting over' undesired frequencies). This contrived silence certainly has benefits, and I have used such headphones on a plane, not so much to listen to music but to help me sleep. They quieten things down, but they do not produce silence. The only true silence is the silence of the grave, as the psalmist puts it: 'The dead do not praise the Lord, nor do any that go down into silence' (Psalm 115:17, NRSV). John refers to silence in heaven for about half an hour when the Lamb opens the seventh seal (Revelation 8:1)—remarkable, considering how many saints and angels praise God continually in that vision of heaven.

Solitude is not about silence, nor does something like silence necessarily create solitude—but solitude can be found in the midst of noise or music, whereas silence cannot. Solitude involves a quietness that pays homage to silence but does not necessarily submit to it. In solitude (as opposed to loneliness) we do not feel alone, and that is why it can involve music—any music.

In solitude, we can relate to God; that is why many seek it. If we include music in our solitude, we have a choice: we can listen to it or we can use it to remove other distractions. If we want to do the latter, we can use almost any piece of music, according to our taste, for its purpose is not musical but eliminatory. This is not wrong, and, if we choose to take this approach, we may well find ourselves alone with God.

If we pay attention to the music, following its contours, admiring its recapitulations and savouring its melody and harmony, we will be in musical companionship with its creator: the composer-in-the-work who decides what we hear and who accompanies us as we journey through the piece. He or she may be a very unassuming, subtle presence, but is there. Similarly, the performers, be it a solo or an orchestra, form the company in which we wish to find a place to be alone with God.

It is therefore nigh on impossible for me to recommend a particular musical piece to aid your solitude! For what I have said does not apply to a particular piece or performance but to how we can use music both in daily life and to aid spiritual contemplation. On a retreat, people often keep silence, which preserves a kind of amiable solitude in which services are attended and meals shared, yet no words are uttered. In that safe but

Solitude can be found

in the midst of noise or music, whereas silence cannot

quiet environment, the detritus of modern living can be put aside, solitude found and God truly encountered. Listen to a piece of music (any you like) and you may find that it can do a similar thing for you, giving you a place where you can be alone with God, wherever you are. ■

Readings for reflection
Psalm 115

Music to listen to

Any piece of music that helps you feel closer to God. Or try 'performing' John Cage's 4'33" (sit in silence and contemplate the sounds around you, as part of God's world). You need not be alone to do this.

The sound of silence

Amy Boucher Pye is a US American who has lived in the UK for over a decade. She makes her home in north London with her husband and young family and enjoys writing and editing for Christian periodicals, including her monthly columns in 'Woman Alive' and 'Christian Marketplace'.

The incongruity of reading a murder mystery during a time set apart for communion with God was finally too much even for me. I packed up *K Is for Killer* in my duffel bag and vowed not to open the zip.

I was at my favourite place of retreat, where I had met God previously. There I had decided against entering a marriage commitment; there I had received a fresh filling of God's Spirit; there had I entered his presence in quiet and gentle ways. This time, however, I felt far from the Lord. I knew in my head that he was there even if I didn't feel his presence, but my heart wasn't so sure.

I had been silent for hours but was not truly quiet; the voices screaming inside drowned out any still, small voice of God. I was filled with pain and doubt. 'Are you really speaking to me, God?' I cried out. 'Is that really *you* I'm hearing, or is it just my heart? Or something else? I don't want to anchor my life on what's not real. Are you there? Can I hear you?'

Anguish had filled me for weeks. I had announced that I was leaving the Christian organization I was working for to join another Christian group in a different city, but my plans had fallen through. Bottomed out, more like it. The opportunities I was pursuing evaporated as the doors slammed in my face. The embarrassment of announcing my intentions and then not leaving was painful, but more devastating was my belief that God had directed the move.

I yearned for God yet couldn't bear to approach him. After a few weeks, however, I knew I needed a place of quiet in which to face the pain and to seek God's solace. Having made arrangements with the retreat centre, I began my time alone with a mixture of fear and anticipation. Yet here I was reading the latest Sue Grafton novel. I came to my senses and lugged my Bible, journal and a blanket down to the nearby pond for a change of scene. After gazing at the serene water and the wildlife around it, I was finally able to pour out my pain, disappointment and confusion to the Lord. In the silence and solitude, he met me; God the Father, God the Son, and God the Holy Spirit surrounded and silenced me with his love and peace. Once again, my heart knew and believed.

It would take many years of growing in maturity before I would be more confident in discerning the still, small voice of God. But that day at the convent was a turning point in my relationship, for once again I was able to trust and receive assurance from him. It was only when I silenced the competing voices and offered up to the Lord my unrealized hopes and dreams that I was able to enter into a deep quiet and hear his voice.

The roar of the stillness

Why is the spiritual discipline of solitude and its close partner, silence, so difficult for us modern people? The answer is seemingly obvious: we have manifold possibilities with which to fill our lives, much of it via technology, such as television, mobile phones and the Internet—blogs, email, chat rooms and the like. Technology surely

> **I knew I needed a place of quiet in which to face the pain and to seek God's solace**

contributes to the cacophony surrounding us, but a deeper answer resides in the condition of the human heart. Blaise Pascal was on to it back before Blackberries® (in the 1600s) when he said that all our miseries derive from not being able to sit alone in a quiet room.

Augustine of Hippo, in a famous line from his *Confessions*, puts it succinctly: 'For you have formed us

> ## We can only survive solitude
> ### if we cling to Christ there

To release those niggles often takes a conscious effort in prayer

for yourself, and our hearts are restless until they find their rest in you.' The God-shaped vacuum inside us cries out to be filled. If we don't turn to God, we will look to something else, such as pulp fiction, food, wine, sex, shopping or even the building of God's kingdom. Turning down the volume of the outside noise and taking away the comfort-crutches leaves us on our own, naked before God. And for many, like me on that day in the convent, that is chilling.

Indeed, silence can be frightening, Dallas Willard says in his fine book *The*

Spirit of the Disciplines (Harper San Francisco, 1990), 'because it strips us as nothing else does, throwing us upon the stark realities of our life. It reminds us of death, which will cut us off from this world and leave only us and God.' He continues, 'In solitude, we confront our own soul with its obscure forces and conflicts that escape our attention when we are interacting with others... We can only survive solitude if we cling to Christ there.'

And that is what I found; when I finished falling, I landed on Christ. Never are there more welcoming arms; never is there a more solid foundation.

'Be still and know'

Many of us run from solitude and silence, but these disciplines are vital to a flourishing and robust spiritual life. Setting aside time in the day, week, month and year to be alone with God will feed our souls as nothing else will. I hear you respond, 'My schedule is already too full—I can't possibly fit in another thing.' As a parent of young children, I can relate. At such stages of life, or, for example, if you're caring for a sick loved one, an offsite retreat may be out of the question.

Richard Foster in his classic *Celebration of Discipline* speaks to this dilemma:

Solitude is more a state of mind and heart than it is a place... If we possess inward solitude we do not fear being alone, for we know that we are not alone. Neither do we fear being with others, for they do not control us. In the midst of noise and confusion we are settled into a deep inner silence. Whether alone or among people, we always carry with us a portable sanctuary of the heart.

He recommends that we make the most of what he calls the 'little solitudes' of the day, such as the early morning before the family awakes, during our morning cuppa, while in traffic or commuting, when we glimpse a tree or a flower. As he says, 'These tiny snatches of time are often lost to us. What a pity! They can and should be redeemed.'

But maybe you are able to get away for a 24-hour (or longer) retreat for silence and solitude. I've always found the best settings to be those nestled in a lovely spot of nature, for there are fewer distractions and the surroundings themselves lead to worship of the Creator. The trees of the wood sing out in joy before the Lord; the sea roars and the fields rejoice. God's handiwork is awe-inspiring and produces a grateful heart.

One of my strong petitions while on retreat (and at other times) is to enter into a deep silence so that I can hear the voice of the Lord and receive from him. I'm easily distracted and, like Martha while Jesus was visiting, 'worried and upset about many things' (Luke 10:41, NIV). For me to release those niggles often takes a conscious effort in prayer, usually through writing out my meditations on a verse of

Scripture or spending time praising the Lord in song. For example, in seeking quietness I might pray through a verse from Isaiah: 'In repentance and rest is your salvation, in quietness and trust is your strength...' (30:15) But sometimes what I need most is simply a nap—and that's the most 'spiritual' thing I can be doing.

Whether we're able to get away for a couple of hours, a couple of days or not at all, the practice of solitude and silence can bring us not only into communion with God but into a newfound freedom. Through it we can

> Why is the spiritual discipline of solitude and its close partner silence **so difficult for us modern people?**

be released from the need to fill our time with words, distractions, self-soothing behaviour or the pressing desire for the approval of others. For when Jesus says, 'Come to me, all you who are weary and burdened, and I will give you rest' (Matthew 11:28), we can believe and know that he is speaking to us.

As we meet with the God of the universe, the One who bids us call him *Abba*, we are changed into his likeness. His presence is beyond compare—far and above any murder mystery. ∎

On retreat

Jim Green is a primary teacher and attends Norwich Vineyard Church, where he oversees children's and youth work and helps with a couple of football teams. He has to deal with the

pains and joys of being a Norwich City supporter, and has a wife and two sons.

Perhaps there are times when you pray
in the hustle and bustle of a high street

'Good morning,' I said. 'I've come to find the answer.'

'Let me know when you've found it,' replied the nun who runs the retreat house I visit; that day at the convent they sounded as if they were seeking some answers of their own! I cycle the few miles from Norwich about three times a year—no expert, just an ordinary(ish) chap wanting to spend some time with God.

Why? I have been looking for what I should do with myself, well, since 1976, when Jesus appeared in my life at university. The search intensified about seven years ago after leaving full-time teaching for supply work, with the hope that this would lead to something more fulfilling. Seven years later, I am still seeking.

Before I set out from home to go on retreat, I have to cross various mental barriers: should I do something more useful, like cleaning our house? Does my wife approve of my going off for the day? (The answer to that is always 'yes'). I go with a mixture of needs. Yes, I would like ongoing direction, but I also have church matters to mull over: children's work, all-age worship, football teams. Then there is just me. Which of these is the day for? It is usually the last that I start with—if I focus too soon on my responsibilities, it feels like work, and I stop.

So what is a typical day like? I arrive at about ten o'clock and usually have a chat with my host. Our conversation is short but important: she is very down to earth and makes me feel at home. I then have a choice of rooms: small and basic with brown furniture or large, with more comfortable, grey furniture. Once that is resolved, I visit the kitchen to make a pot of tea. I am more relaxed than on my early visits, when I was apprehensive at the thought of meeting an unknown nun or guest. Now I feel more at home, and I am often the only guest there.

As well as necessary refreshment, my tea drinking is a security blanket, a rest before I consider the delightful impossibility of the day. I mean, I'm here to spend time with God. How on earth do I do that? The delight is in aspiring to what I know I can't do. Always I sit, close my eyes, pray, read the Bible. I don't have a programme. 'Hang the world, give me a river,' sang the Christian songwriter Martyn Joseph, and that includes 'hanging' techniques and methods of getting somewhere. It is more or less a day in an armchair, when I try to focus—or just doze. Of course, a walk in the grounds would keep me awake but my cycling gives me quite enough exercise. Anyway, I am happy with dozing: if it is dozing with

God, what is wrong with that?

Sometimes I have flicked through the magazines and books in the room, although I am genuinely unsure whether this helps. On the one hand, it would be a foolish man who could assert that he had nothing to learn, for instance, from Mother Julian of Norwich, but it sometimes feels as if I flit uneasily from booklet to book, hoping for some inspiration that would set me up for the day. I do not often feel that I find it, but perhaps that is because I know what I am after: a day is a short enough time without wasting it looking for help from a book when I should be looking to God himself.

Sometimes I will kneel or lie in a posture of submission but that is usually a brief intermission from the armchair, and on my return my movement is limited to pulling myself upright and rearranging the cushion once I have slid down too far to be comfortable. Is that all? Yes, and it is an unbelievably wonderful rest: this armchair is my place for the day.

Lunchtime arrives. Initially I joined the Sisters for their silent lunch but I felt a little uncomfortable, perhaps because I didn't see the point

Always I sit, close my eyes, pray, read the Bible. **I don't have a programme**

... it would be a foolish man who could assert that he had nothing to learn in eating in silence with strangers, so now I bring my own and eat it—yes, in the armchair. This is also definitely time for a break from being spiritual. It's time, if possible, for an enjoyable novel or, failing that, the sports section of the *Guardian* or *Eastern Daily Press*.

It's the afternoons when things seem to happen. I don't know whether that's because the disappearing day panics me into greater focus or because it takes that time to adjust or for God to get through to me. Whatever, I have usually finished reading by this stage and am more intent on engaging with God.

If I get round to praying about my responsibilities, I always end up with people: picturing them and feeling for them. One way or another I

> ## God appears to be touching a hidden part of me

> ### Taking myself out of the daily routine for a few hours is good in itself

never consider decisions about 'projects'. It tends to be quiet prayer, too; if I was on a deserted, wide beach with noisy surf I could make as much noise as I like, but I'm in a house where there might be others around, so I

adapt and am quiet. I enjoy this: the restraint on my mouth cuts down the words and allows space for feeling to grow—not emotion, not passion, just feeling. What I am feeling for is not as important as the fact that God appears to be touching a hidden part of me. What dominates is stillness, a sense of rest, of trust. Peace.

I leave at about half past four in the afternoon, usually wishing I could stay longer. My lips have been more or less closed for a day and I don't want to open them. Happily, my cycle ride home starts through gentle countryside, so my quiet day does not end as soon as I leave the convent.

How has it gone?

I would love to report that I regularly hear a recognizable answer, a voice saying, 'Do this or that', directing my life, but to be honest I don't expect it—and I am still supply teaching. It seems to me that taking myself out of the daily routine for a few hours is good in itself. It is good for my wife, my sons, those whom I serve, that I have sought to spend a day with God.

I never come away thinking that I should have cleaned the house instead. ∎

Breathing spaces
on the pilgrim journey

Richard Woodham is an Anglican clergyman, husband, father and grandfather who lives by the River Bure in Norfolk. After serving as a parish priest and youth officer, he now promotes outdoor spirituality, encourages pilgrimage and works for the Small Pilgrim Places Network.

In a strange city, reeling from her mother's death, Jenny sought sanctuary in the cathedral church. There was nothing wrong with the cathedral. It was full of life. Preparations were being made for a service and the place was busy with tourists. The restlessness in that great building matched her inner restlessness. She could not settle, so she walked the streets of the city until providence brought her to a small ancient church with an open door. She went in.

Sitting in the quiet, she let the atmosphere of peace breathe into her. In time, she found her heart beating in unison with whatever it was that lived

She could not settle

and breathed in that place. She 'calmed and quieted [her] soul, like a weaned child with its mother' (Psalm 131:2, NRSV).

Once her time of praying was over, she got into conversation with a person at the back of the church who had sensitively given her the space she needed. She discovered that the church—St Pancras, Exeter—was a member of Small Pilgrim Places Network. As a response, she joined the network as a supporter, convinced that every city should have at least one.

Many visitors were affected by what they encountered

Parking at Poldhu Cove, beneath a blue sky and white scudding clouds, I took the Cornish Coastal Path over the headland. The sky was mirrored in a sea with white-topped waves. Wild flowers abounded—bluebells, wild garlic, thrift, sea campion and golden gorse. Above, a raven and buzzard disputed territory and newly arrived swallows swooped after fresh hatchings of mayflies.

Over the hill, the first sight of St Winwaloe's Church revealed it as a perfect location for a fifth-century monastery. It was sheltered from the weather by the bulk of a hill and built on the banks of a stream where it discharged fresh water into the salty sea. Nothing of the original church remains, but the freestanding bell tower is said to incorporate the original hermit's cave. (If you were to go there,

you could park in the National Trust car park at Church Cove.)

Descending into the cove and crossing the stream, I arrived at the church's south door, where a modern statue of the saint stood in welcome. The door was open and, as I went in and adjusted to the dim light, I noticed that it was beautifully kept. A deep, still prayerfulness infused the building, in sharp contrast to the wild wind, waves and sunshine outside. As I sat and reflected, I noted a steady stream of visitors—some came to wander and wonder, others to sit and pray.

Later, as I looked through the visitors' book and the book for prayers, it was clear how many visitors were affected by what they encountered. St Winwaloe's is a place where praying comes easy! It would be quite appropriate to place a sign outside claiming, as Jacob said of Bethel, 'This is none other than the house of God, and this is the gate of heaven' (Genesis 28:17).

The same verse is placed above the door of the church at Little Gidding, in Cambridgeshire. Inspired by this place, T.S. Eliot was moved to express a truth, which has much to say about visiting such places of pilgrimage:

You are here to kneel
Where prayer has been valid...

These are places where time and eternity come together:

Here, the intersection of the
timeless moment
Is England and nowhere.
Never and always.
FROM 'LITTLE GIDDING', NO. 4 OF *FOUR QUARTETS*

Both St Winwaloe's and Little Gidding also belong to the Small Pilgrim Places Network.

Not every place in the network is an ancient building. The Yurt, which is the mobile focus of Breathing Space arts ministry, has a temporary resting space in the back garden of a house in New Barnet, one of London's northern suburbs.

There is nothing new about small pilgrim places; they have always existed. Like spiritual wi-fi hotspots, they are found in every land and in the care of a wide range of people and groups. By way of contrast, the Small Pilgrim Places Network is new and not yet far-flung.

The Revd Jim Cotter wrote to US American friends in 2000 about a project he had embarked upon in Wales: 'A small church in a small community in a small country on the north-western edges of Europe. A place that attracts pilgrims who may be doubling as tourists, or indeed disguised as such.' His plan was to open the little-used St Tecwyn's Church at Llandecwyn, on the hills above Porthmadog, as a small pilgrim place and to exercise a ministry of welcome.

'How can we change the glazed eyes of the tourist within each of us into the focused eyes of the pilgrim?' Jim had mused. People of all faiths and none found their way to the church's newly reopened doors. The beauty of its setting, the silence, stillness and a sense of presence worked its miracle on many. It also deeply affected Jim and the volunteers who staffed the church during summer months. Offering hospitality to those who lived nearby as well as to summer visitors, they found themselves earthed in the local community and woven across time with St Tecwyn, the hermit who founded the church, and with subsequent generations of worshippers into the fabric of the communion of saints.

The message given
by locked doors is far from that of the open arms of Christ

It occurred to Jim that, although Llandecwyn was unique, small pilgrim places, which come in all shapes and sizes, had many things in common—uniqueness being but one! There was, it seemed, much that could be gained if those who had the care of SPPs and wanted to exercise a ministry of welcome worked together—sharing experience, know-how, wisdom and publicity and offering mutual support. So the idea of a Small Pilgrim Place Network was born.

Formally launched in Birmingham on 8 October 2005, the network adopted a provisional constitution and objectives and offered those who joined a provisional good practice guide.

Defining what is, and what is not, a small pilgrim place was not immediately easy. Places like Canterbury Cathedral, Lourdes or Walsingham are clearly big pilgrimage places but even within big places there may be hidden, humble and holy places that are 'off the beaten track' and so open to membership. The network's website carries this definition:

• Places with presence, where it's easy to meditate, think and pray
• The ancient Celts sometimes described such places as 'thin';

others used the word 'liminal'— thresholds on the edge of mystery
• Often they are ancient places of worship, still pools of quiet in the midst of restless cities, wayside shrines, prayer stations on a pilgrim path, stone circles, holy wells, quiet gardens…
• They may be the home or last resting place of a saint or poet
• They will feel like spiritual oases, somewhere to take stock and take breath

Good practice requires that each SPP appoints what the network terms a 'hospitaller'—someone with the responsibility of welcoming visitors.

Different SPPs have different needs and a different level of resources. Sometimes a hospitaller will appoint deputies, and a team of hospitallers will share the ministry of welcome. Occasionally, it is necessary or desirable for a hospitaller or deputy to be in attendance whenever the place is open. Often someone next door or further afield will be able to fill the role well enough.

Differences apart, all SPPs that are members of the network will:

- welcome people of goodwill regardless of colour, creed or gender
- attend to the spiritual needs of both place and people
- not be pushy or preachy
- offer simple hospitality, quiet prayer and thoughtful conversation

There is a real need in this fast-moving, 24–7, noisy and restless postmodern society for quiet places close to the still centre of the turning world. Even in our homes we find ourselves continually stimulated by radio, television and all the stuff that comes to us through our computers, iPods and mobile phones. Where are we to find places to 'come away… and rest a while' (Mark 6:31) without the danger of being sold something? Where can a modern-day Elijah find a cave in which to listen to the still small voice?

The vocation to be a Small Pilgrim Place can give remote rural churches and those in the city a new lease of life and a new focus to their mission— a 'fresh expression', to use a current phrase! Leaving a church locked from Sunday to Sunday might be an easier path, but the message given by locked doors is far from that of the open arms of Christ.

Finally, a true story: the hospitallers got used to the figure of Win as she sneaked into church in the early afternoon. After a period of weeks she was ready to speak. Two things were happening in her life: the first was the reawakening of her spiritual life; the second was the return of a virulent cancer and an illness that would prove to be terminal.

She joined a confirmation group where she gave as much as she received, infectiously spreading the new fire that had sprung up in her. Her confirmation and first Communion were in the hospital bed where she was to die a few days later. Remembering Win, I marvel at how she remained so

> Even in our homes we find
> ourselves continually stimulated

full of life and joy right to the end.

'Do not neglect to show hospitality to strangers,' says the author of Hebrews, 'for by doing that some have entertained angels…' (13:2). Everything I have come to know confirms this as good advice! ∎

To find out more about Small Pilgrim Places and the network, visit www.smallpilgrimplaces.org. Alternatively, you can write to Richard Woodham at 40 Anchor Street, Coltishall, Norfolk NR12 7AQ.

United with the Lord Almighty

Susan Rand is on the board of Release International and has travelled to meet those suffering for their faith in Iran, Nigeria and Sri Lanka. She lives in Bicester with her husband Stephen. They have two grown-up daughters and delight in their two grandchildren.

My husband and I have just moved to a town where we know no one. During the day, I am alone in the house for hours at a time. Some days I have felt lonely, but mainly this has been a time of solitude. I know it is not going to last—we are getting to know people and rekindling old friendships with those who live nearby.

Many people will choose to take a day apart from their usual activity to spend time in solitude. It may be time for God; it may be time for some personal space. Equally, there is a long spiritual tradition, which continues today, of pursuing a calling to solitude and quietness. For Richard Wurmbrand,

however, it was very different: his solitude was not a choice.

Richard Wurmbrand was born a Romanian Jew in 1909. Brought up in a non-religious home, he became a convinced atheist. As a young married couple, he and his wife, Sabina, converted to Christianity and became church leaders. During the Second World War, they were arrested and beaten by the Nazi occupation force in Romania on several occasions. In 1944, Russian troops invaded and set up a communist regime that forced the church underground. Richard was arrested in 1948 and Sabina soon after. Sabina was sent to the Danube canal where she worked as a slave labourer for three years; Richard was put into solitary confinement.

For three years, he saw no one except his gaolers and torturers, who wore soft shoes so he could not hear their approach. He was 30 feet underground. He could not see daylight; he lost all sense of colour—everything was grey. He had neither a Bible nor any other books, and, with no paper or writing implements, he forgot how to write.

After those years alone, he was transferred to a cell with other prisoners, but the torture continued for a further five years. During much of this time, his family believed him to be dead. Released in 1957, he was rearrested in 1959 and sentenced to a further 25 years in prison. Following a general amnesty in 1964, he was released once again but, fearing a third imprisonment, Norwegian Christians negotiated with the Romanian government and paid a ransom for him, allowing him and his family to leave the country. This was not his choice, but other leaders in the underground church urged him to take the opportunity to leave and tell the West what was happening.

Once in the West, Richard founded Christian Mission to the Communist World (later to be called Release International) to bring support to those persecuted for their faith in communist countries and other regimes hostile to Christians, and he wrote many books in both English and Romanian, including the bestselling Tortured for Christ. After moving to live in the USA, he and his wife travelled the world, working tirelessly for religious liberties.

In 1990, after the fall of Ceausescu, Richard and Sabina returned to Romania. Warmly received, he was invited to preach on television. Government officials offered the use of the Ceausescu palace cellars, the very place where Richard had been in solitary confinement, as a storage facility for Christian books and printing presses. He died in 2001, Sabina predeceasing him by a few months.

In 1966, soon after his arrival in the West, Richard gave testimony to the US Senate Judiciary Committee. He said,

He had no Bible

but he had prepared himself beforehand by memorizing it

'For years I have never seen sun, moon, flowers, snow, stars, no man except the interrogator who beat me. But I can say I have seen heaven open, I have seen Jesus Christ, I have seen the angels, and we were very happy there.'

How did he find happiness in those years of enforced solitude? The key for him was spiritual discipline—and the key to spiritual discipline was preparation. He had no Bible but he had prepared himself beforehand by memorizing it. He would recall it to

mind and 'read' it to himself, meditating on the verses before preparing sermons, one each day. With no congregation to hear his sermons, he would deliver them beginning with 'Dear brothers and sisters' and ending with 'Amen'. He learnt these sermons by using short rhymes to help his memory and, on his release, he was able to recall 350 of them, some of which can be read in his book *With God in Solitary Confinement*. There were times, after prolonged torture, when he would forget everything and, on occasion, the only word of the Lord's Prayer he could remember was 'Father'. But as he recovered, it all came flooding back.

He rarely thought about the tortures themselves, but focused on matters unrelated to the pain. He said in another book, *100 Prison Meditations*: 'We were free to rejoice in the mysteries of the word of God. With such things we kept busy.' He slept during the day and woke as other prisoners were going to sleep, quoting Psalm 134:1 (NIV) to himself: 'Praise the Lord, all you servants of the Lord who minister by night in the house of the Lord.' He believed that because demonic forces were more at work in the dark hours, he should be awake and praying. During those night hours he would pray for the whole world, country by country, and for any town or person that he happened to know of in each country. He would pray for whatever situations he could think of—families eating together, couples getting married—and he would rejoice with them.

Ultimately, Richard Wurmbrand's spiritual discipline was not about mind games or even spiritual exercises. It was about complete dependence on the living Christ. Part of it was the recognition that he was in a situation in which nothing could be relied upon; in prison, everything was removed. Faith that depended on

> He saw no one except his gaolers and torturers

anything other than Jesus would fail. In *The Triumphant Church*, he wrote: 'Nobody resists who has not renounced the pleasures of life beforehand.'

He insisted that there was a deeper reality to be grasped, one that was not to be found in comforting Bible verses. He provocatively said that God never meant Psalm 23 to strengthen Christians: 'It is the Lord who can strengthen you, not the Psalm which speaks of him so doing. It is not enough to have the Psalm. You must have the One about whom the Psalm speaks' (*The Triumphant Church*). What he learnt from his enforced solitude was that 'if you are united with the Reality, the Lord Almighty, evil loses its power over you; it cannot break the Lord Almighty'. Such was his sense of that reality that he could say, 'I thank God for the years which I passed in solitary confinement.' ■

The Northumbria Community:

Mulling over the questions

Trevor Miller is a Baptist minister and an overseer of the Northumbria Community based at the Community's Mother House at Hetton Hall, Northumberland.

'Can you tell me a little about yourselves? What is the Northumbria Community?' These and many like them are frequently asked questions, which are not always easy to answer, not least because the Northumbria Community describes a network of people, hugely diverse, from different backgrounds, streams and edges of the Christian faith.

Those who are Companions in Community are united in their desire to embrace an ongoing exploration into a new way for living Christianly that offers hope in the changed and changing cultures of today's world. Each has to learn to translate and apply our *Way for Living*—centred on availability and vulnerability before God and others—to their own situations and circumstances, as each has to face differing roles, responsibilities and relationships. This commitment to adaptability and flexibility makes it very difficult to translate our life adequately into words. The best we can do is to talk about living the questions at the heart of our life as a response rather than an answer. Answers give finality, whereas we want to convey life still being lived, discoveries yet to be made, exploration and adventure being real.

This is why the Northumbria Community is always in draft form, and, because it is dynamic, organic and ongoing, it is never a finished product.

There are some unchanging principles and core values, however, in that the essence of the Northumbria Community ethos is found in each Companion. Each can say, 'This is what I am, who I am,' and these are like the words in a stick of seaside rock—embedded throughout, part of the thing itself so that however much it is broken up, the letters remain. Ideally, for Companions, the life and message have become who they are; it is in the heart, not in knowledge alone.

From our earliest days as a Community we have understood that two concepts capture this essence, both seen in the original meaning of the old Greek word *ethos*—both the atmosphere ('ether') and the habitual practices ('ethics') of any group within that atmosphere. We recognize that the 'ether' in which we live, move and have our being today is that of a rapidly changing culture, characterized by a consumer-driven, instant-communication globalism. Exploring how to live in this new world, our 'ethics' (seen in our core values and spiritual disciplines) enabled us to discover our *Way for Living*. This is embodied in living constantly with three questions: Who is it you seek? How then shall we live? How shall we sing the Lord's song in a strange land?

The Community is geographically dispersed and strongly ecumenical but has an identity rooted in the history and spiritual heritage of Celtic Northumbria. Our continuing quest for a new monasticism is the heart of our life, whether alone or together. It is this blending of 'a prayer that is quiet and contemplative and a faith

... a new way for living Christianly that offers hope

that is active and contagious' (as stated in our 1989 foundational document), lived out in the ordinariness of everyday life, which forms the basis for our growth and development.

This came alive in the merging of two groupings in the late 1980s—the Nether Springs Trust (contemplative and prophetic) and Northumbria Ministries (apostolic and missionary) —which was the major turning point in the establishment of the Northumbria Community and the single most important event following the early pioneering years that had began a decade before.

A spirituality that offers simplicity, solitude and contemplative awareness

Living the questions at the heart of our life

We discovered that to seek God for his own sake is never just an intellectual exercise: it is life lived in the ordinary and mundane. We are all seekers and always remain so—hence the continual question, 'Who is it you seek?' that lies at the heart of our ethos. 'Who is it you seek?' is our message, giving voice to our mission, which is not only to create the space to seek God in our own lives but also to help others clearly led by God along parallel paths. Many people (like us) are suffering an interior homelessness; they are internal émigrés. Many are aware of being in exile, often bewildered by the huge winds of change shaping our culture and yet, despite it all, clearly on pilgrimage with hope in their hearts. Our discovery of a new monastic spirituality, strongly influenced by the way of life expressed in the monastic communities at Roslin in Scotland and at Clonfert in Ireland, enables us to live with such hope.

God's call on the Northumbria Community is not to any form of institutionalism but to explore monastic spirituality in the ordinariness of our lives as a different way of relating to today's world. We believe that we are experiencing as a Community (along with many others) a holy restlessness and a divine concern regarding the nature of faith, which has only begun to make sense of the nonsense within us and around us through an embracing of monastic values and disciplines. Monastic spirituality implies a single-hearted (solitary) seeking of God. This may or may not be carried out in the company of others (the monastic tradition has embraced both being alone and being together), but the focus is on returning to God. It also involves making use of a daily rhythm of prayer (Office) and a *Way for Living* (Rule). These enable us to marry the inner journey, the landscape of the heart—a call to repent, to deny ourselves, and to recognize and resist evil—with the outer journey, the landscape of the land, which has given us a platform to find a different way of being church. We can then offer the fruit of our life to all who come our way, asking with them, 'Who is it you seek? How then shall we live? How shall we sing the Lord's song in a strange land?'

Our Mother House, the Nether Springs, is situated quite deliberately in north Northumberland as a fulfilment of Joshua 15:17–19, a foundational scripture about the Father's gift to us of both the Nether Springs and the Upper Springs. In the early days, this passage inspired us to seek for 'the nether springs'. Holy Island was clearly the place of the Upper Springs; but somewhere further inland would be a place where people could seek the nether, hidden, deeper springs of spirituality rooted in the history and heritage of Northumbria.

This scripture became a source of hope—hope that, as the pioneers walked away from familiar territory, a way would be found for the journey ahead. They travelled in the hope that the journey was not in vain but was at God's invitation and would be sustained by God's provision. The Nether Springs is the hidden place, not simply geographically but in relation to our spirituality as well. It is a place where individuals come to seek God on their own journey of faith. It is a well from which seekers can draw water to sustain them in their journey with God.

Our Mother House holds the heart of the Community's life insofar as it is a symbol of the Community's vocation to seek God as the 'one thing necessary' (see Luke 10:42). Life at the Mother House is shaped around a daily rhythm of work, worship, study, community and solitude. This offers a gentle structure that turns our attention towards God even in the midst of ordinary life. At the centre of this rhythm is the Daily Office, shared in our chapel in the gardens of the house.

As a Community, we offer time, resources, understanding, validation and support for all who are genuinely seeking God. We want to be there for all those who have discovered an inner reality of 'being' alongside 'doing'; who long, in the words of T.S. Eliot, for 'a still point in a turning world'. They need a spirituality that offers simplicity, solitude and contemplative awareness in a busy and noisy world, yet still acknowledges the reality of that world where we have to live our lives.

It is this single-minded search for God which, being essentially

> **... turns our attention** towards God even in the midst of the ordinariness of life

monastic, stands in the tradition of wisdom that is not an accumulation of knowledge for its own sake but is about a constant application of it to life. As the saying goes: 'A wise person does not gather and dispense insights, but rather has the heart to live those insights'. ■

Solitude

Sister Stephanie-Thérèse is a member of the Community of the Sisters of the Love of God, an Anglican contemplative order of nuns in Oxford. She has been with the community since 1988 and is currently working with their publishing ministry, the SLG Press.

Each Bible reading is an example of God's interaction with one of his servants while they are on their own or with Jesus when he is alone. They represent the counterbalance to corporate worship, showing the fruitfulness of time alone with God.

Each prayer contains three sections. The first addresses God and brings our attention to him. Contemplate this first section, go back and reread the Bible verse (or related passage in the Bible) and think about the interaction between God and his servant. What can God teach us in these encounters? The second section ('Let us…') again places us before God, this time in

response to the essence of the reading. Pick out the key word(s) and ponder them. How can these words strengthen our response to God? The third section is a simple petition of what comes out of this reflection on the Bible text. What do we desire in our lives, arising from these readings?

Sunday

Solitude and encounter

When Moses went up on the mountain, the cloud covered it, and the glory of the Lord settled on Mount Sinai. For six days the cloud covered the mountain, and on the seventh day the Lord called to Moses from within the cloud (Exodus 24:15–16, NIV).

Loving Father, in the cloud upon the mountain you talked with Moses face to face as to a friend. Let our solitude be the mountain where we encounter your glory. Give us fortitude for the ascent and an open heart to receive your presence.

Monday

Solitude and response

Samuel was lying down in the temple of the Lord, where the ark of God was... The Lord came and stood there, calling... 'Samuel! Samuel!' Then Samuel said, 'Speak, for your servant is listening' (1 Samuel 3:3, 10, abridged).

Loving Father, you sought out Samuel in the temple and called him to your service. Let our solitude become a place of readiness and response. Grant us the grace to answer your call at once, with joy and with the whole of our hearts.

Tuesday

Solitude and waiting

And there [Elijah] came to a cave, and lodged there... And behold, the Lord passed by... a great strong wind... an earthquake... a fire, but the Lord was not in [these]; and after the fire a still small voice. And when Elijah heard it, he wrapped his face in his mantle and went out and stood at the entrance of the cave (1 Kings 19:9a, 11b–13, RSV).

Loving Father, you tested Elijah, alone in a cave, with wind and earthquake and fire. Let our solitude be a place of waiting. Teach us patience in the testing, and discernment to recognize your voice, and in the stillness and the smallness, let us stand and draw closer to you.

Wednesday

Solitude and selfishness

'Now, O Lord, take away my life, for it is better for me to die than to live.' But the Lord replied, 'Have you any right to be angry?' Jonah went out and sat down at a place east of the city. There he made for himself a shelter, sat in its shade and waited... (Jonah 4:3–5a, NIV).

Loving Father, you showed us in your servant Jonah that our response to your will can be selfish and defiant. Let our solitude be a place of self-knowledge and growth. Give us the courage, when we run away and hide, to turn to you and relinquish our self-centred thoughts and desires, that with purity of heart and mind we may again seek to do your will.

Friday

Solitude and intercession

But when you pray, go into your room, close the door and pray to your Father, who is unseen. Then your Father, who sees what is done in secret, will reward you (Matthew 6:6).

Loving Father, your Son taught us to withdraw and pray to you in secret. Let the closed door of our solitude never shut out the world and its needs. Make our heart and mind steadfast so that our prayer is not deflected by the trifling allurements of wandering thoughts.

Let us find a place of solitude in the midst of this world's busyness...

Saturday

Solitude and communion

And after [Jesus] had dismissed the crowds, he went up on the mountain by himself to pray (Matthew 14:23, RSV).

Loving Father, your only Son withdrew from his ministry to be alone with you in prayer. Let us find a place of solitude in the midst of this world's busyness. Help us to seek that still place of your presence where we can be with you and praise you and learn from you, so that we return to our daily lives with renewed enthusiasm and wisdom.

Thursday

Solitude and temptation

At once the Spirit sent [Jesus] out into the desert, and he was in the desert for forty days, being tempted by Satan. He was with the wild animals, and angels attended him (Mark 1:12–13).

Loving Father, your only Son was tempted by Satan in the wilderness. Let our solitude be a place of spiritual strength to resist the enticements of evil. Minister to us and strengthen us in the time of trial and let us find you in the struggle and in the victory.

Musings of a middle-aged mystic

Veronica Zundel is a journalist, author and contributor to 'New Daylight'. She has also written 'The Time of our Lives' (2007) and 'Crying for the Light' (2008) for BRF. She lives in north London.

Somewhere among my possessions, I still have a rather moving letter that a fellow university student wrote to me after our first and only date. He explained very nicely that, while he liked my company, he felt that God had called him to be alone. I took him at his word. The only trouble is, within hardly more than a year he was married to someone else! His call to solitude seems to have been remarkably temporary...

Solitude can be a tempting prospect when our lives are too busy or when relationships seem too complicated. It can also be essential for us to be alone with God, to seek perspective and to refresh our spirits. Some view the prospect of being alone with horror. I certainly had too much of it when I was living alone and working freelance at home: days could go by without my speaking to anyone at all. Others, such as mothers of small children (which I have also been), dream of a few moments of solitude as a blessed relief.

But what is the difference between solitude and loneliness? And does fruitful solitude have to be voluntary, or can we still gain spiritually from an enforced solitude? I suspect that really to benefit from solitude, we have to like ourselves and like God—two

To make an uncrowded space where we can fully encounter our own selves

visitors a day who were seeking their wisdom; Julian had a window in her cell that opened on to the outside and people would go there regularly to seek her advice, as her fellow mystic Margery Kempe did. I think, too, of Sister Wendy Beckett, a hermit who has written in this issue of *Quiet Spaces*. She spends seven hours a day in prayer, yet she has also used her art history training to become a popular television presenter. I sometimes suspect that hermits have a busier social life than I, writing at home, do!

What really is the point of seeking solitude? Ultimately it's not to 'get away from everything'. It's to make an uncrowded space where we can fully encounter our own selves, with all our flaws and abilities; where we can experience God's love; and where we can confront the needs of the world in prayer. Some of us can manage a brief 'quiet time' once a day or more; some need to take a more focused time away from daily life, for instance on a retreat; some are called to a sustained solitude, whether officially as a hermit or informally as a single person living alone.

Whatever our level of solitude, we all, at some time in our lives, need to step back from chatter and company, from work and worry, and to be alone with our God. The person who has truly learnt—and it may take a long time—to benefit from solitude will never be lonely. And, because solitude teaches us to be still, to wait and to listen, that person will probably be better company. ■

achievements which are possibly connected. Nothing could be worse than to hate one's own company, unless it's to have the wrong kind of fear of God, the kind that makes us want to avoid God's gaze. Perhaps, though, solitude is the surest way of discovering we have either or both of these problems, and beginning to address them.

Solitude, of course, doesn't have to be constant, permanent or total. I am intrigued by hermits such as the Desert Fathers, or Julian of Norwich a thousand years later. Hermits used to receive sometimes as many as ten

Do take a moment to visit the Quiet Spaces website (www.quietspaces.org.uk) and email us with your thoughts, perhaps sparked by what you have read in this issue.

In our next issue

'No man is an island,' said John Donne. 'There is no such thing as society,' said Margaret Thatcher. 'All the believers were one in heart and mind. No one claimed that any of their possessions was their own, but they shared everything they had,' wrote Luke (Acts 4:21, TNIV). The next issue of *Quiet Spaces* will consider what 'community' can and should mean for Christians today. Is it a comfortable 'belonging' or a radical challenge?

Contact us at:

Quiet Spaces,
BRF,
15 The Chambers,
Vineyard, Abingdon
OX14 3FE
enquiries@brf.org.uk

BRF Quiet Days

Jesus himself said, 'Come away and rest a while.'

BRF offers a programme of themed Quiet Days held at locations across the UK. A Quiet Day is an ideal way of redressing the balance in our busy lives. It provides focus and inspiration from an experienced speaker and allows spaces in which to be silent and at rest, to allow God to speak to us through his word, his creation and his still, small voice.

The cost of a BRF Quiet Day is usually £20–£25, including lunch. Special offer: bring four friends to any day and get the fifth place free!

The *Quiet Days and Events* e-news is sent out every other month, and features a preview of upcoming Quiet Days as well as input from speakers, recommended resources and a chance to give your feedback. To join this mailing list, email us on events@brf.org.uk or visit our website: www.quietspaces.org.uk.

All our Quiet Days are listed at www.quietspaces.org.uk. For more information, you may also contact Ceri Ellis on ceri.ellis@brf.org.uk or 01865 319709.